# 13x9 PAN

## CASSEROLES, DESSERTS AND MORE

Publications International, Ltd.

**Pictured on the front cover:** Easy Chicken Chalupas (page 28).

**Pictured on the back cover** (top to bottom): Chicken and Asparagus Casserole
(page 36) and Hearty Potato and Sausage Bake (page 44).

ISBN: 978-1-4508-9153-0

Library of Congress Control Number: 2014938646

Manufactured in China.

8 7 6 5 4 3 2 1

Publications International, Ltd.

# TABLE OF CONTENTS

## Cheddar and Leek Strata

- 8 eggs
- 2 cups milk
- ½ cup porter or stout
- 2 cloves garlic, minced
- ½ teaspoon salt
- ¼ teaspoon black pepper
- 1 loaf (16 ounces) sourdough bread, cut into ½-inch cubes
- 2 small leeks, coarsely chopped
- 1 red bell pepper, chopped
- 1½ cups (6 ounces) shredded Swiss cheese
- 1½ cups (6 ounces) shredded sharp Cheddar cheese

**1.** Spray 13×9-inch baking dish with nonstick cooking spray. Whisk eggs, milk, porter, garlic, salt and black pepper in large bowl until well blended.

**2.** Spread half of bread cubes in prepared baking dish. Sprinkle with half of leeks and half of bell pepper. Top with ¾ cup Swiss cheese and ¾ cup Cheddar cheese. Repeat layers. Pour egg mixture evenly over top.

**3.** Cover tightly with plastic wrap or foil. Weigh top of strata down with slightly smaller baking dish. Refrigerate at least 2 hours or overnight.

**4.** Preheat oven to 350°F. Bake, uncovered, 40 to 45 minutes or until center is set. Serve immediately.                *Makes 12 servings*

# Date-Nut Granola

2 cups old-fashioned oats
2 cups barley flakes
1 cup sliced almonds
⅓ cup vegetable oil
⅓ cup honey
1 teaspoon vanilla
1 cup chopped dates

**1.** Preheat oven to 350°F. Spray 13×9-inch baking pan with nonstick cooking spray.

**2.** Combine oats, barley flakes and almonds in large bowl. Combine oil, honey and vanilla in small bowl. Pour honey mixture over oat mixture; mix well. Pour into prepared pan.

**3.** Bake about 25 minutes or until toasted, stirring frequently after first 10 minutes. Stir in dates while mixture is still hot. Cool completely. Store tightly covered. *Makes 6 cups*

**Tip:** It's easy to change this recipe to suit your taste. Swap out the almonds for chopped pecans or walnuts, and use raisins, dried cranberries and/or chopped dried apricots instead of dates.

# Aunt Marilyn's Cinnamon French Toast Casserole

  1  large loaf French bread, cut into 1½-inch slices

3½  cups milk

  9  eggs

1½  cups granulated sugar, divided

  1  tablespoon vanilla

 ½  teaspoon salt

  6  to 8 baking apples, such as McIntosh or Cortland, peeled and sliced

  1  teaspoon ground cinnamon

 ½  teaspoon ground nutmeg

    Powdered sugar (optional)

**1.** Spray 13×9-inch baking dish with nonstick cooking spray. Arrange bread slices in single layer in prepared dish.

**2.** Whisk milk, eggs, 1 cup granulated sugar, vanilla and salt in large bowl until well blended. Pour half of mixture over bread. Layer apple slices over bread. Pour remaining half of egg mixture over apples.

**3.** Combine remaining ½ cup granulated sugar, cinnamon and nutmeg in small bowl; sprinkle over casserole. Cover and refrigerate overnight.

**4.** Preheat oven to 350°F. Bake, uncovered, 1 hour or until set. Sprinkle with powdered sugar, if desired. *Makes 6 to 8 servings*

# Cinnamon Raisin Rolls

      1   package (16 ounces) hot roll mix, plus ingredients
            to prepare mix
     ⅓   cup raisins
      4   tablespoons (½ stick) butter, softened, divided
     ¼   cup granulated sugar
      2   teaspoons ground cinnamon
     ½   teaspoon ground nutmeg
   1½   cups powdered sugar
      1   to 2 tablespoons milk
     ½   teaspoon vanilla

**1.** Preheat oven to 375°F. Spray 13×9-inch baking pan with nonstick cooking spray.

**2.** Prepare hot roll mix according to package directions; stir in raisins. Knead dough on lightly floured surface about 5 minutes or until smooth and elastic. Cover and let rest 5 minutes.

**3.** Roll out dough into 16×10-inch rectangle. Spread 2 tablespoons butter over dough. Combine granulated sugar, cinnamon and nutmeg in small bowl; sprinkle evenly over dough. Starting with long side, roll up dough jelly-roll style. Pinch seam to seal.

**4.** Gently stretch rolled-up dough to 18 inches in length. Cut crosswise into 1-inch slices; place slices cut sides up in prepared pan. Cover loosely and let rise 20 to 30 minutes or until doubled in size.

**5.** Bake rolls 20 to 25 minutes or until golden brown. Cool in pan on wire rack 3 minutes; remove to wire rack.

**6.** Whisk powdered sugar, remaining 2 tablespoons butter, 1 tablespoon milk and vanilla in medium bowl until smooth. Add additional milk, 1 teaspoon at a time to thin glaze, if necessary. Spread glaze over warm rolls.

*Makes 18 rolls*

# Ranchero Egg Bake

   1   pound ground pork sausage
   1   can (4 ounces) ORTEGA® Diced Green Chiles
   ½  cup water
   1   packet (1.25 ounces) ORTEGA® Taco Seasoning Mix
   1   package (12-count) ORTEGA® Yellow Corn Taco Shells, divided
   1   can (15 ounces) ORTEGA® Black Beans, rinsed, drained
   2   cups (8 ounces) shredded Cheddar or taco cheese
 10   eggs, lightly beaten
   1   cup ORTEGA® Salsa, any variety
   1   cup milk

**Preheat** oven to 350°F.

**Brown** sausage in large skillet over medium heat, stirring to separate meat as it cooks. Add chiles, water and seasoning mix. Set aside.

**Crush** 10 taco shells coarsely; spread on bottom of 13×9-inch casserole pan. Sprinkle beans evenly over taco shells. Spread meat mixture evenly on top. Sprinkle cheese evenly over meat.

**Combine** eggs, salsa and milk in medium mixing bowl. Pour over casserole ingredients. Crush remaining 2 taco shells; sprinkle evenly over casserole. Bake 45 minutes.                                    *Makes 12 servings*

**Prep Time:** 15 minutes
**Start to Finish Time:** 60 minutes

# Apple Cream Cheese Breakfast Bars

## Crust

- 1 package (about 15 ounces) yellow cake mix
- ¼ teaspoon grated lemon peel
- ½ cup (1 stick) butter, softened

## Filling

- 12 ounces cream cheese, softened
- ½ cup sugar
- 2 eggs
- ½ cup half-and-half
- 2 teaspoons vanilla

## Topping

- ⅓ cup sugar
- 1 teaspoon ground cinnamon
- 1 teaspoon ground nutmeg
- ¼ teaspoon grated lemon peel
- 2½ cups thinly sliced Granny Smith apples (2 medium)
- ½ cup sliced almonds

**1.** Preheat oven to 350°F. Combine cake mix and ¼ teaspoon lemon peel in large bowl. Reserve ½ cup mixture for filling. Add butter to remaining mixture; beat with electric mixer at low speed until crumbly. Press onto bottom and up sides of ungreased 13×9-inch baking pan. Bake 10 minutes or until lightly browned.

**2.** Beat cream cheese and reserved ½ cup cake mix in large bowl with electric mixer at medium speed until well blended. Gradually add ½ cup sugar; beat until creamy. Add eggs, one at a time, beating well after each addition. Beat in half-and-half and vanilla until blended. Pour into baked crust.

**3.** Combine ⅓ cup sugar, cinnamon, nutmeg and ¼ teaspoon lemon peel in large bowl. Add apples; toss to coat. Spoon apple mixture over cream cheese layer; sprinkle with almonds.

**4.** Bake 30 to 35 minutes or until center is set. Cool completely in pan on wire rack. Cut into bars.

*Makes 24 bars*

# Blueberry Crumb Cake

Crumb Topping (recipe follows)
2 cups all-purpose flour
⅔ cup sugar
1 tablespoon baking powder
1 teaspoon salt
½ teaspoon baking soda
1 cup milk
½ cup (1 stick) butter, melted
2 eggs
2 tablespoons lemon juice
2 cups fresh or thawed frozen blueberries

**1.** Preheat oven to 375°F. Spray 13×9-inch baking pan with nonstick cooking spray. Prepare Crumb Topping.

**2.** Sift flour, sugar, baking powder, salt and baking soda into large bowl. Combine milk, butter, eggs and lemon juice in medium bowl. Add to flour mixture; stir until well blended.

**3.** Pour batter into prepared pan. Sprinkle blueberries evenly over batter; sprinkle with Crumb Topping.

**4.** Bake 40 to 45 minutes or until toothpick inserted into center comes out clean. Serve warm. *Makes 12 to 16 servings*

**Crumb Topping:** Combine 1 cup chopped walnuts or pecans, ⅔ cup sugar, ½ cup all-purpose flour, ¼ cup (½ stick) softened butter and ½ teaspoon ground cinnamon in large bowl until mixture forms coarse crumbs.

# Hash Brown Casserole

1 package (32 ounces) frozen Southern-style hash brown potatoes, thawed

1 container (16 ounces) sour cream

1 can (10¾ ounces) condensed cream of chicken soup, undiluted

1½ cups (6 ounces) shredded sharp Cheddar cheese

¾ cup thinly sliced green onions

4 slices bacon, crisp-cooked and crumbled

2 teaspoons hot pepper sauce

¼ teaspoon garlic salt

**1.** Preheat oven to 350°F. Spray 13×9-inch baking pan with nonstick cooking spray.

**2.** Combine potatoes, sour cream, soup, cheese, green onions, bacon, hot pepper sauce and garlic salt in large bowl; mix well. Spoon into prepared pan.

**3.** Bake 55 to 60 minutes or until potatoes are tender and cooked through. Stir before serving. *Makes 12 servings*

# Chocolate Chunk Coffeecake

1¾ cups all-purpose flour
1 teaspoon baking powder
1 teaspoon baking soda
½ teaspoon salt
¾ cup packed brown sugar
½ cup (1 stick) butter, softened
3 eggs
1 teaspoon vanilla
1 cup sour cream
1 package (about 11 ounces) semisweet chocolate chunks
1 cup chopped nuts

**1.** Preheat oven to 350°F. Spray 13×9-inch baking pan with nonstick cooking spray.

**2.** Combine flour, baking powder, baking soda and salt in medium bowl. Beat brown sugar and butter in large bowl with electric mixer at medium speed until creamy. Add eggs and vanilla; beat until well blended. Alternately add flour mixture and sour cream; beat until blended. Stir in chocolate chunks and nuts. Spread batter evenly in prepared pan.

**3.** Bake 25 to 35 minutes or until toothpick inserted into center comes out clean. Cool in pan on wire rack.                    *Makes 12 to 16 servings*

# Breakfast Bake

1 pound ground pork sausage

1 teaspoon Italian seasoning

½ teaspoon salt

6 eggs

2 cups milk

½ cup CREAM OF WHEAT® Hot Cereal (Instant, 1-minute, 2½-minute or 10-minute cook time), uncooked

1 teaspoon TRAPPEY'S® Red Devil™ Cayenne Pepper Sauce

4 cups cubed bread stuffing (potato bread recommended)

2 cups shredded Cheddar cheese

**1.** Brown sausage in skillet, pressing with fork or spatula to crumble as it cooks. Sprinkle with Italian seasoning and salt; set aside.

**2.** Combine eggs, milk, Cream of Wheat and pepper sauce in large mixing bowl; mix well. Add cooked sausage and bread stuffing; toss to combine. Pour mixture into 13×9-inch casserole pan; cover. Refrigerate at least 4 hours or overnight.

**3.** Preheat oven to 350°F. Remove cover and sprinkle cheese over casserole. Cover pan with aluminum foil; bake 30 minutes. Remove foil; bake 15 minutes longer. Serve warm.                                                 *Makes 8 servings*

**Prep Time:** 30 minutes
**Start to Finish Time:** 4 to 12 hours soaking, 45 minutes baking

**Serving Suggestion:** Serve this dish with a salad and some fresh fruit on holiday mornings or for a special brunch.

## Sunday Dinner Casserole

2 cups egg noodles, cooked and drained
2 pounds boneless skinless chicken breasts
2 cups sliced sweet onions
½ cup dry sherry
2 tablespoons sugar
2 tablespoons balsamic vinegar
1 teaspoon dried thyme
½ teaspoon black pepper
3 cups chicken broth
1 can (about 14 ounces) diced tomatoes
2 cloves garlic, minced
½ teaspoon red pepper flakes
¼ cup chopped fresh basil
2 teaspoons grated lemon peel

**1.** Preheat oven to 400°F. Spray 13×9-inch baking dish with nonstick cooking spray.

**2.** Place noodles in prepared baking dish. Top with chicken.

**3.** Combine onions, sherry, sugar, vinegar, thyme and black pepper in large skillet; cook and stir over medium heat until onions begin to brown. Stir in broth, tomatoes, garlic and red pepper flakes until well blended. Pour over chicken.

**4.** Bake 20 minutes. Turn chicken; bake 20 to 25 minutes or until chicken is no longer pink in center. Sprinkle with basil and lemon peel.

*Makes 4 to 6 servings*

# Turkey Cutlets with Stuffing & Cranberries

1 bag (14 ounces) PEPPERIDGE FARM® Cubed Herb
   Seasoned Stuffing

1 stick butter

1 stalk celery, chopped (about ½ cup)

1 medium onion, chopped (about ½ cup)

1¾ cups SWANSON® Chicken Stock

1 can (16 ounces) whole cranberry sauce

8 turkey breast cutlets (about 2 pounds)

1 can (10¾ ounces) CAMPBELL'S® Condensed Cream of Chicken
   Soup (Regular **or** 98% Fat Free)

⅓ cup milk

**1.** Crush **1 cup** stuffing to make coarse crumbs. Set aside.

**2.** Heat the butter in a large saucepot over medium heat. Add the celery and onion and cook until they're tender. Add the stock. Heat to a boil. Remove from the heat. Add the remaining stuffing and stir lightly to coat.

**3.** Spoon the stuffing mixture into 13×9×2-inch baking pan. Spread the cranberry sauce over the stuffing. Top with the turkey.

**4.** Stir the soup and milk in a small bowl. Pour evenly over the turkey. Sprinkle with the reserved stuffing crumbs.

**5.** Bake at 375°F. for 1 hour 5 minutes or until the turkey is cooked through.

*Makes 8 servings*

**Kitchen Tips:** If turkey cutlets are not available, purchase whole turkey London broil (about 2 pounds) and cut into 8 cutlets.

The recipe can be prepared and fully cooked the day before. To reheat, cover and bake at 375°F. for 1 hour and 10 minutes or until hot.

# Easy Chicken Chalupas

1 rotisserie chicken (about 2 pounds)
8 (8-inch) flour tortillas
2 cups (8 ounces) shredded Cheddar cheese
1 cup mild green salsa
1 cup mild red salsa

**1.** Preheat oven to 350°F. Spray 13×9-inch baking dish with nonstick cooking spray.

**2.** Shred chicken; discard skin and bones.

**3.** Place 2 tortillas in prepared baking dish, overlapping slightly. Layer tortillas with 1 cup chicken, ½ cup cheese and ¼ cup of each salsa. Repeat layers three times.

**4.** Bake 25 minutes or until bubbly and heated through.

*Makes 6 servings*

**Tip:** Serve this easy main dish with toppings such as sour cream, chopped cilantro, sliced black olives, sliced green onions and sliced avocado.

# Creamy Chicken and Pasta with Spinach

6 ounces uncooked egg noodles

2 boneless skinless chicken breasts (about 12 ounces), cooked and cut into 1-inch pieces

1 package (10 ounces) frozen chopped spinach, thawed and drained

1 can (4 ounces) sliced mushrooms, drained

1 tablespoon olive oil

¼ cup chopped onion

¼ cup chopped red bell pepper

2 cups (8 ounces) shredded Swiss cheese

1 cup sour cream

¾ cup half-and-half

2 eggs

½ teaspoon salt

**1.** Preheat oven to 350°F. Spray 13×9-inch baking dish with nonstick cooking spray. Cook noodles according to package directions; drain and place in large bowl. Add chicken, spinach and mushrooms; mix well.

**2.** Heat oil in medium skillet over medium-high heat. Add onion and bell pepper; cook and stir 2 minutes or until onion is tender. Add to chicken mixture.

**3.** Combine cheese, sour cream, half-and-half, eggs and salt in medium bowl; mix well. Add to chicken mixture; stir until blended. Spoon into prepared baking dish. Cover with foil.

**4.** Bake 30 to 35 minutes or until heated through.     *Makes 6 to 8 servings*

# Southwest Turkey Bake

1  pound ground turkey
1  can (about 15 ounces) black beans, rinsed and drained
1  cup salsa
½  teaspoon ground cumin
⅛  teaspoon ground red pepper
1  package (about 8 ounces) corn muffin mix
¾  cup reduced-sodium chicken broth
1  egg
¾  cup (3 ounces) shredded Mexican cheese blend

**1.** Preheat oven to 400°F. Spray 13×9-inch baking dish with nonstick cooking spray.

**2.** Cook turkey in large nonstick skillet over medium-high heat until no longer pink, stirring to break up meat. Stir in beans, salsa, cumin and red pepper; simmer 2 minutes. Spoon into prepared baking dish.

**3.** Combine corn muffin mix, broth and egg in medium bowl; mix well. Spread over turkey mixture. Sprinkle with cheese.

**4.** Bake 15 minutes or until edges are lightly browned.

*Makes 6 to 8 servings*

# Chipotle Chicken Enchiladas

2 cans (10 ounces each) ORTEGA® Enchilada Sauce, divided

2 cups shredded cooked chicken

1 cup ORTEGA® Refried Beans

1 packet (1.25 ounces) ORTEGA® Chipotle Taco Seasoning Mix

8 (8-inch) ORTEGA® Flour Soft Tortillas

1 cup (4 ounces) shredded Mexican-blend cheese

**Preheat** oven to 350°F. Lightly coat 13×9-inch baking dish with nonstick cooking spray. Spread ½ can enchilada sauce on bottom of dish.

**Combine** chicken, 1 can enchilada sauce, beans and seasoning mix in medium skillet over medium-low heat. Cook and stir 3 to 4 minutes or until mixture is heated through.

**Wrap** tortillas with clean, lightly moistened cloth or paper towels. Microwave on HIGH (100% power) 1 minute or until hot and pliable. Spoon chicken mixture evenly down center of each tortilla; roll up. Place in prepared dish, seam side down. Top evenly with remaining ½ can enchilada sauce and cheese.

**Bake** 15 to 20 minutes or until heated through and cheese is melted. Serve warm.                         *Makes 8 enchiladas*

**Prep Time:** 10 minutes
**Start to Finish Time:** 30 minutes

# Chicken Asparagus Casserole

1 tablespoon vegetable oil

1 cup chopped green and/or red bell peppers

1 medium onion, chopped

2 cloves garlic, minced

1 can (10¾ ounces) condensed cream of asparagus soup, undiluted

1 container (8 ounces) ricotta cheese

2 cups (8 ounces) shredded Cheddar cheese, divided

2 eggs

1½ cups chopped cooked chicken

1 package (10 ounces) frozen chopped asparagus,* thawed and drained

8 ounces egg noodles, cooked and drained

Black pepper (optional)

*Or substitute ½ pound fresh asparagus cut into ½-inch pieces. Bring 6 cups water to a boil in large saucepan over high heat. Add asparagus; cover and cook over medium heat 5 to 8 minutes or until crisp-tender. Drain.*

**1.** Preheat oven to 350°F. Spray 13×9-inch baking dish with nonstick cooking spray.

**2.** Heat oil in medium skillet over medium heat. Add bell peppers, onion and garlic; cook and stir until vegetables are crisp-tender.

**3.** Combine soup, ricotta cheese, 1 cup Cheddar cheese and eggs in large bowl; mix well. Add onion mixture, chicken, asparagus and noodles; stir until well blended. Season with black pepper, if desired.

**4.** Spread mixture evenly in prepared baking dish. Top with remaining 1 cup Cheddar cheese.

**5.** Bake 30 minutes or until center is set and cheese is bubbly. Let stand 5 minutes before serving. *Makes 6 to 8 servings*

# Chicken Chilaquiles

Salsa Chipotle (recipe follows)
12 (6- or 7-inch) corn tortillas
1 tablespoon vegetable oil, divided
2 cups shredded cooked chicken
6 eggs, beaten
1 cup (4 ounces) shredded Chihuahua or Manchego cheese
½ cup finely crumbled queso añejo or feta cheese

**1.** Prepare Salsa Chipotle. Preheat oven to 375°F. Spray 13×9-inch baking dish with nonstick cooking spray.

**2.** Place tortillas in single stack on cutting board; cut into ½-inch-wide strips. Heat 1½ teaspoons oil in large skillet over medium-high heat until shimmering. Add half of tortilla strips; cook until golden brown, stirring frequently to separate tortilla strips. Remove to prepared baking dish with slotted spoon. Repeat with remaining tortilla strips, adding remaining oil if necessary. Add chicken and salsa to baking dish; toss gently to coat. Stir in eggs.

**3.** Cover with foil and bake 35 minutes or until tortillas are soft but not soggy and casserole is heated through. Sprinkle with Chihuahua cheese. Bake, uncovered, 5 to 10 minutes or until cheese is melted and casserole is beginning to brown. Cool 5 minutes before serving. Sprinkle each serving with queso añejo. *Makes 6 to 8 servings*

**Salsa Chipotle:** Combine 1 (28-ounce) can whole tomatoes, drained, and 2 canned chipotle peppers in blender; pulse to purée. Heat 1 tablespoon vegetable oil in large saucepan over medium heat. Add ½ large white onion, cut into ¼-inch slices; cook and stir until golden brown. Add 3 cloves minced garlic; cook and stir 1 minute. Add tomato mixture; cook about 5 minutes or until mixture boils and thickens. Stir in 2½ cups chicken broth. Remove from heat; cool to room temperature. Stir in additional broth to make 4½ cups total, if necessary. Stir in ½ cup finely chopped fresh cilantro. Season with salt.

# Chicken Cassoulet

  4  slices bacon
  ¼  cup all-purpose flour
      Salt and black pepper
1¾  pounds bone-in chicken pieces
  2  chicken sausages (2¼ ounces each), cooked and cut into ¼-inch pieces
  1  medium onion, chopped
1½  cups diced red and green bell peppers
  2  cloves garlic, minced
  1  teaspoon dried thyme
  1  teaspoon olive oil
  2  cans (about 15 ounces each) cannellini or Great Northern beans, rinsed and drained
  ½  cup dry white wine (optional)

**1.** Preheat oven to 350°F. Cook bacon in large skillet over medium-high heat until crisp; drain on paper towel-lined plate. Cut into 1-inch pieces. Pour off all but 2 tablespoons drippings from skillet.

**2.** Place flour in shallow bowl; season with salt and black pepper, if desired. Dip chicken pieces in flour mixture; shake off excess. Brown chicken in batches in skillet over medium-high heat; remove to plate. Lightly brown sausages in same skillet; remove to plate.

**3.** Add onion, bell peppers, garlic and thyme to skillet; cook and stir over medium heat 5 minutes or until softened, adding oil as needed to prevent sticking. Add beans; mix well. Spoon into 13×9-inch baking dish. Top with chicken, sausages and bacon. Add wine to skillet, if desired; cook and stir over medium heat, scraping up browned bits from bottom of skillet. Pour over chicken.

**4.** Cover and bake 40 minutes. Uncover; bake 15 minutes or until chicken is cooked through (165°F). *Makes 6 servings*

# Chicken Zucchini Casserole

1 package (about 6 ounces) herb-flavored stuffing mix
½ cup (1 stick) butter, melted
2 cups cubed zucchini
1½ cups chopped cooked chicken
1 can (10¾ ounces) condensed cream of celery soup, undiluted
1 cup grated carrots
1 onion, chopped
½ cup sour cream
½ cup (2 ounces) shredded Cheddar cheese

**1.** Preheat oven to 350°F. Combine stuffing mix and butter in medium bowl; reserve 1 cup stuffing. Place remaining stuffing in 13×9-inch baking dish.

**2.** Combine zucchini, chicken, soup, carrots, onion and sour cream in large bowl; mix well. Pour over stuffing in baking dish; top with reserved 1 cup stuffing and cheese.

**3.** Bake 40 to 45 minutes or until heated through and cheese is melted.

*Makes 6 to 8 servings*

## Hearty Potato and Sausage Bake

- 1 pound new red potatoes, cut into halves or quarters
- 1 onion, sliced
- ½ pound baby carrots
- 2 tablespoons butter, melted
- 1 teaspoon salt
- 1 teaspoon garlic powder
- ½ teaspoon dried thyme
- ½ teaspoon black pepper
- 1 pound cooked chicken sausage or turkey sausage, cut into ¼-inch slices

**1.** Preheat oven to 400°F. Spray 13×9-inch baking dish with nonstick cooking spray.

**2.** Combine potatoes, onion, carrots, butter, salt, garlic powder, thyme and pepper in large bowl; toss to coat. Spoon into prepared baking dish.

**3.** Bake 30 minutes. Stir in sausage; bake 15 to 20 minutes or until potatoes are tender and golden brown.           *Makes 4 to 6 servings*

# Chili Spaghetti Casserole

     8  ounces uncooked spaghetti
     1  pound ground beef
     1  medium onion, chopped
    ¼  teaspoon salt
    ⅛  teaspoon black pepper
     1  can (about 15 ounces) vegetarian chili with beans
     1  can (about 14 ounces) Italian-style stewed tomatoes, undrained
  1½  cups (6 ounces) shredded sharp Cheddar cheese, divided
    ½  cup sour cream
  1½  teaspoons chili powder
    ¼  teaspoon garlic powder

**1.** Preheat oven to 350°F. Spray 13×9-inch baking dish with nonstick cooking spray.

**2.** Cook spaghetti according to package directions; drain and place in prepared baking dish.

**3.** Meanwhile, combine beef, onion, salt and pepper in large skillet; cook over medium-high heat 6 to 8 minutes or until browned, stirring to break up meat. Drain fat. Stir in chili, tomatoes with juice, 1 cup cheese, sour cream, chili powder and garlic powder.

**4.** Add chili mixture to spaghetti; stir until well coated. Sprinkle with remaining ½ cup cheese. Cover with foil.

**5.** Bake 30 minutes or until hot and bubbly. Let stand 5 minutes before serving. *Makes 6 to 8 servings*

# Family-Style Frankfurters with Rice and Beans

  1   tablespoon vegetable oil
  1   onion, chopped
  ½   green bell pepper, chopped
  2   cloves garlic, minced
  1   can (about 15 ounces) black beans, rinsed and drained
  1   can (about 15 ounces) Great Northern beans, rinsed and drained
  8   ounces beef frankfurters, cut into ¼-inch pieces
  1   cup uncooked instant brown rice
  1   cup vegetable broth
  ¼   cup packed brown sugar
  ¼   cup ketchup
  3   tablespoons dark molasses
  1   tablespoon Dijon mustard

**1.** Preheat oven to 350°F. Spray 13×9-inch baking dish with nonstick cooking spray.

**2.** Heat oil in large saucepan over medium-high heat. Add onion, bell pepper and garlic; cook and stir 3 minutes or until tender.

**3.** Add beans, frankfurters, rice, broth, brown sugar, ketchup, molasses and mustard to saucepan; stir gently until blended. Spoon into prepared baking dish. Cover with foil.

**4.** Bake 30 minutes or until rice is tender.          *Makes 6 to 8 servings*

# Beef Stroganoff Casserole

- 1 pound ground beef
- ¼ teaspoon salt
- ⅛ teaspoon black pepper
- 1 tablespoon vegetable oil
- 8 ounces sliced mushrooms
- 1 large onion, chopped
- 3 cloves garlic, minced
- ¼ cup dry white wine
- 1 can (10¾ ounces) condensed cream of mushroom soup, undiluted
- ½ cup sour cream
- 1 tablespoon Dijon mustard
- 4 cups cooked egg noodles
- Chopped fresh parsley (optional)

**1.** Preheat oven to 350°F. Spray 13×9-inch baking dish with nonstick cooking spray.

**2.** Combine beef, salt and pepper in large skillet; cook over medium-high heat 6 to 8 minutes or until browned, stirring to break up meat. Drain fat. Transfer to bowl.

**3.** Heat oil in same skillet over medium-high heat. Add mushrooms, onion and garlic; cook and stir 2 minutes or until onion is tender. Stir in wine; simmer 3 minutes over medium-low heat. Remove from heat; stir in soup, sour cream and mustard until well blended. Return beef to skillet; mix well.

**4.** Place noodles in prepared baking dish. Pour beef mixture over noodles; stir until noodles are well coated.

**5.** Bake 30 minutes or until heated through. Sprinkle with parsley, if desired.

*Makes 6 to 8 servings*

# Hearty Lasagna Rolls

1½   pounds ground beef
  1   cup chopped fresh mushrooms
  1   medium onion, finely chopped
  1   small carrot, finely chopped
  1   clove garlic, finely chopped
  ¼   cup dry red wine or beef broth
  ⅛   teaspoon cayenne pepper (optional)
  2   cups shredded mozzarella cheese
  1   egg, lightly beaten
  5   tablespoons grated Parmesan cheese, divided
  1   jar (1 pound 8 ounces) RAGÚ® Robusto!® Pasta Sauce
 12   ounces lasagna noodles, cooked and drained

**1.** Preheat oven to 350°F. In 12-inch skillet, brown ground beef over medium-high heat; drain. Stir in mushrooms, onion, carrot and garlic; cook over medium heat, stirring occasionally, until vegetables are tender. Stir in wine and cayenne pepper; cook over high heat 3 minutes. Remove from heat; let stand 10 minutes.

**2.** In medium bowl, thoroughly combine ground beef mixture, mozzarella cheese, egg and 2 tablespoons Parmesan cheese. In 13×9-inch baking dish, evenly pour 2 cups Pasta Sauce. Evenly spread ⅓ cup ground beef filling over each lasagna noodle. Carefully roll up noodles. Place seam side down in baking dish. Evenly spread remaining Sauce over lasagna rolls. Bake, covered, 40 minutes. Sprinkle with remaining 3 tablespoons Parmesan cheese and bake, uncovered, 5 minutes or until bubbling.

*Makes 6 servings*

# Sausage Pizza Pie Casserole

8  ounces mild Italian sausage, casings removed

1  package (about 14 ounces) refrigerated pizza dough

½  cup tomato sauce

2  tablespoons chopped fresh basil *or* 2 teaspoons dried basil

½  teaspoon dried oregano

¼  teaspoon red pepper flakes

3  ounces mushrooms, quartered

½  cup thinly sliced red onion

½  cup thinly sliced green bell pepper

½  cup seeded diced tomato

½  cup sliced pitted black olives

8  slices smoked provolone cheese

2  tablespoons grated Parmesan or Romano cheese

**1.** Preheat oven to 350°F. Spray 13×9-inch baking dish with nonstick cooking spray.

**2.** Cook sausage in large nonstick skillet over medium-high heat 6 to 8 minutes or until browned, stirring to break up meat. Drain fat.

**3.** Unroll pizza dough in prepared baking dish; press evenly onto bottom and up sides of dish. Spoon tomato sauce evenly over dough; sprinkle with basil, oregano and red pepper flakes. Layer with sausage, mushrooms, onion, bell pepper, tomato, olives and provolone cheese. Roll down sides of crust to form rim.

**4.** Bake 20 to 25 minutes or until crust is golden brown. Sprinkle with Parmesan cheese; let stand 5 minutes before serving.

*Makes 4 to 6 servings*

# Fiesta Beef Enchiladas

- 1 pound ground beef
- ½ cup sliced green onions
- 2 teaspoons minced garlic
- 1½ cups chopped tomatoes, divided
- 1 cup cooked white or brown rice
- 1 cup (4 ounces) shredded Mexican cheese blend or Cheddar cheese, divided
- ¾ cup frozen corn, thawed
- ½ cup salsa or picante sauce
- 12 (6- to 7-inch) corn tortillas
- 1 can (10 ounces) enchilada sauce
- 1 cup shredded romaine lettuce

**1.** Preheat oven to 375°F. Spray 13×9-inch baking dish with nonstick cooking spray.

**2.** Cook beef in medium nonstick skillet over medium-high heat 6 to 8 minutes or until browned, stirring to break up meat. Drain fat. Add green onions and garlic; cook and stir 2 minutes. Remove from heat; stir in 1 cup tomatoes, rice, ½ cup cheese, corn and salsa.

**3.** Spoon mixture down center of tortillas. Roll up tortillas and filling; place seam side down in prepared baking dish. Spoon enchilada sauce evenly over enchiladas. Cover with foil.

**4.** Bake 20 minutes or until heated through. Sprinkle with remaining ½ cup cheese; bake, uncovered, 5 minutes or until cheese melts. Top with lettuce and remaining ½ cup tomatoes. *Makes 6 servings*

# Beefy Pasta Casserole

- 1 pound ground beef
- 1 tablespoon dried oregano leaves, crushed
- 2 cans (10¾ ounces **each** ) CAMPBELL'S® Condensed Tomato Soup (Regular **or** Healthy Request®)
- 1 soup can water
- ½ of a 16 ounce package (4 cups) **uncooked** corkscrew-shaped pasta (rotini)
- 1 container (15 ounces) ricotta cheese
- 1 cup shredded mozzarella cheese (4 ounces)

**1.** Cook the beef and oregano in a 12-inch skillet over medium-high heat until the beef is well browned, stirring frequently to separate meat. Pour off any fat.

**2.** Stir the soup, water and pasta in a 13×9×2-inch (3-quart) shallow baking dish. Add the beef mixture and ricotta cheese and stir to coat. **Cover.**

**3.** Bake at 375°F. for 30 minutes or until hot and bubbly. Sprinkle with the mozzarella cheese. Let stand for 5 minutes or until the cheese melts.

*Makes 6 servings*

**Prep Time:** 15 minutes
**Bake Time:** 30 minutes
**Stand Time:** 5 minutes

# Reuben Noodle Bake

8 ounces uncooked egg noodles

5 ounces thinly sliced deli-style corned beef

2 cups (8 ounces) shredded Swiss cheese

1 can (about 14 ounces) sauerkraut with caraway seeds, drained

½ cup Thousand Island dressing

½ cup milk

1 tablespoon prepared mustard

2 slices pumpernickel bread

1 tablespoon butter, melted

**1.** Preheat oven to 350°F. Spray 13×9-inch baking dish with nonstick cooking spray. Cook noodles according to package directions; drain.

**2.** Meanwhile, cut corned beef into bite-size pieces. Combine noodles, corned beef, cheese and sauerkraut in large bowl; mix well. Spoon into prepared baking dish.

**3.** Combine dressing, milk and mustard in small bowl. Spoon evenly over noodle mixture.

**4.** Tear bread into large pieces; process in food processor until crumbs form. Add butter; pulse to combine. Sprinkle over casserole.

**5.** Bake 25 to 30 minutes or until heated through.    *Makes 6 to 8 servings*

# Mexican Lasagna

1 pound ground beef
1 package (1¼ ounces) taco seasoning mix
1 can (about 14 ounces) Mexican-style diced tomatoes
1½ teaspoons chili powder
1 teaspoon ground cumin
½ teaspoon salt
½ teaspoon red pepper flakes
2 cups (16 ounces) sour cream
1 can (4 ounces) diced mild green chiles, drained
6 green onions, chopped
6 (8-inch) flour tortillas
1 can (15 ounces) corn, drained
2 cups (8 ounces) shredded Cheddar cheese

**1.** Preheat oven to 350°F. Spray 13×9-inch baking dish with nonstick cooking spray.

**2.** Combine beef and taco seasoning in large skillet; cook over medium heat 6 to 8 minutes or until browned, stirring to break up meat. Drain fat.

**3.** Combine tomatoes, chili powder, cumin, salt and red pepper flakes in medium bowl; mix well. Combine sour cream, chiles and green onions in large bowl.

**4.** Layer one third of tomato mixture, two tortillas, one third of sour cream mixture, one third of beef mixture, one third of corn and one third of cheese in prepared casserole. Repeat layers twice.

**5.** Bake 35 minutes or until bubbly. Let stand 15 minutes before serving.

*Makes 6 to 8 servings*

# Spicy Manicotti

    3  cups ricotta cheese
    1  cup grated Parmesan cheese, divided
    2  eggs, lightly beaten
 2½  tablespoons chopped fresh parsley
    1  teaspoon dried Italian seasoning
  ½  teaspoon garlic powder
  ½  teaspoon salt
  ½  teaspoon black pepper
    1  pound spicy Italian sausage, casings removed
    1  can (28 ounces) crushed tomatoes
    1  jar (26 ounces) marinara sauce
    8  ounces uncooked manicotti pasta shells

**1.** Preheat oven to 375°F. Spray 13×9-inch baking dish with nonstick cooking spray.

**2.** Combine ricotta cheese, ¾ cup Parmesan cheese, eggs, parsley, Italian seasoning, garlic powder, salt and pepper in medium bowl; mix well.

**3.** Cook sausage in large skillet over medium-high heat 6 to 8 minutes or until browned, stirring to separate meat. Remove to paper towel-lined plate. Drain fat from skillet.

**4.** Add tomatoes and marinara sauce to same skillet; bring to a boil over high heat. Reduce heat to low; simmer, uncovered, 10 minutes. Pour about one third of sauce into prepared baking dish.

**5.** Fill each pasta shell with about ½ cup ricotta mixture. Place in baking dish. Top shells with sausage and remaining sauce. Cover with foil.

**6.** Bake 50 minutes to 1 hour or until pasta is tender. Let stand 5 minutes before serving. Sprinkle with remaining ¼ cup Parmesan cheese.

*Makes 8 servings*

# Hearty Noodle Casserole

1  pound Italian sausage, casings removed
1  jar (26 ounces) pasta sauce
2  cups (16 ounces) ricotta or cottage cheese
1  package (12 ounces) extra wide egg noodles, cooked
   and drained
2  cups (8 ounces) shredded mozzarella cheese, divided
1  can (4 ounces) sliced mushrooms, drained
½  cup chopped green bell pepper

**1.** Preheat oven to 350°F. Spray 13×9-inch baking dish with nonstick cooking spray.

**2.** Cook sausage in large skillet over medium-high heat 6 to 8 minutes or until browned, stirring to break up meat. Drain fat.

**3.** Combine sausage, pasta sauce, ricotta cheese, noodles, 1 cup mozzarella cheese, mushrooms and bell pepper in large bowl; mix well. Spoon into prepared baking dish. Top with remaining 1 cup mozzarella cheese.

**4.** Bake 25 minutes or until heated through.          *Makes 6 to 8 servings*

## Creamy Pumpkin Baked Penne

- 1 package (14½ ounces) multigrain penne
- 1 tablespoon olive oil
- 1 onion, chopped
- 3 cloves garlic, minced
- 1 can (28 ounces) crushed tomatoes
- 1 can (15 ounces) solid-pack pumpkin
- ¾ cup ricotta cheese
- ½ cup vegetable broth
- 1 tablespoon dried Italian seasoning
- ¾ teaspoon red pepper flakes
- 1 cup (4 ounces) shredded mozzarella cheese
- ⅓ cup grated Parmesan cheese

**1.** Preheat oven to 375°F. Spray 13×9-inch baking dish with nonstick cooking spray.

**2.** Cook pasta according to package directions until al dente; drain.

**3.** Heat oil in large saucepan over medium-high heat. Add onion and garlic; cook and stir 3 minutes. Add tomatoes, pumpkin, ricotta cheese, broth, Italian seasoning and red pepper flakes; bring to a boil. Reduce heat to medium-low; simmer 5 minutes. Stir in pasta. Spoon into prepared baking dish; sprinkle with mozzarella and Parmesan cheeses.

**4.** Bake 30 to 35 minutes or until golden brown.     *Makes 6 to 8 servings*

# Chiles Rellenos Casserole

  3  eggs, separated
 ¾  cup milk
 ¾  cup all-purpose flour
 ½  teaspoon salt
  1  tablespoon butter
 ½  cup chopped onion
  2  cans (7 ounces each) whole green chiles, drained
  8  slices (1 ounce each) Monterey Jack cheese, cut into halves
     Toppings: sour cream, sliced green onions, sliced olives,
     guacamole and salsa

**1.** Preheat oven to 350°F. Spray 13×9-inch baking dish with nonstick cooking spray.

**2.** Combine egg yolks, milk, flour and salt in food processor or blender; process until smooth. Pour into large bowl; set aside.

**3.** Melt butter in small skillet over medium heat. Add onion; cook and stir until tender.

**4.** Pat chiles dry with paper towels. Slit each chile lengthwise and carefully remove seeds. Place two halves of cheese slices and 1 tablespoon onion in each chile; reshape chiles to cover cheese. Place in single layer in prepared baking dish.

**5.** Beat egg whites in medium bowl with electric mixer at medium-high speed until soft peaks form; fold into egg yolk mixture. Pour over chiles in baking dish.

**6.** Bake 20 to 25 minutes or until puffed and knife inserted into center comes out clean. *Turn oven to broil.* Broil 4 inches from heat source 30 seconds or until golden brown. Serve with desired toppings.

*Makes 4 servings*

# Party Potatoes

1 package (32 ounces) Southern-style hash browns

2 cans (10¾ ounces each) condensed cream of potato soup, undiluted

2 cups (16 ounces) sour cream

2 cups (8 ounces) shredded Cheddar cheese

¾ cup finely chopped red onion

¼ cup (½ stick) butter, cut into pieces

Parmesan cheese (optional)

**1.** Preheat oven to 350°F. Spray 13×9-inch baking dish with nonstick cooking spray.

**2.** Combine hash browns, soup, sour cream, Cheddar cheese and onion in large bowl; mix well. Spoon into prepared baking dish; pat down. Dot with butter; sprinkle with Parmesan cheese, if desired. Cover with foil.

**3.** Bake 50 minutes. Uncover and bake 20 minutes or until browned.

*Makes 10 servings*

**Tip:** Serve these rich potatoes as part of a brunch spread along with a frittata and fresh fruit. Or bring this dish to a potluck or tailgate party—it's a recipe that's easy to prepare and pleases just about everyone!

# Three Cheese Baked Ziti with Spinach

- 1 package (16 ounces) **uncooked** medium tube-shaped pasta (ziti)
- 1 bag (6 ounces) baby spinach, washed (about 4 cups)
- 1 jar (1 pound 7 ounces) PREGO® Marinara Italian Sauce
- 1 cup ricotta cheese
- 4 ounces shredded mozzarella cheese (about 1 cup)
- ¾ cup grated Parmesan cheese
- ½ teaspoon garlic powder
- ¼ teaspoon ground black pepper

**1.** Prepare the pasta according to the package directions. Add the spinach during the last minute of the cooking time. Drain the pasta and spinach well in a colander. Return them to the saucepot.

**2.** Stir the Italian sauce, ricotta, **½ cup** of the mozzarella cheese, **½ cup** of the Parmesan cheese, garlic powder and black pepper into the pasta mixture. Spoon the pasta mixture into a 13×9-inch shallow baking dish. Sprinkle with the remaining mozzarella and Parmesan cheeses.

**3.** Bake at 350°F. for 30 minutes or until the mixture is hot and bubbling.

*Makes 6 servings*

**Prep Time:** 15 minutes
**Bake Time:** 30 minutes
**Total Time:** 45 minutes

**Kitchen Tip:** Save valuable time by putting together the casserole a day or less in advance, covering and refrigerating it to bake later.

# Mexican Tortilla Stack-Ups

1 tablespoon vegetable oil

½ cup chopped onion

1 can (about 15 ounces) black beans, rinsed and drained

1 can (about 14 ounces) Mexican- or Italian-style diced tomatoes

1 cup frozen corn

1 package (1¼ ounces) taco seasoning mix

6 (6-inch) corn tortillas

2 cups (8 ounces) shredded Mexican cheese blend

1 cup water

Sour cream (optional)

Sliced black olives (optional)

**1.** Preheat oven to 350°F. Spray 13×9-inch baking dish with nonstick cooking spray.

**2.** Heat oil in large skillet over medium-high heat. Add onion; cook and stir 3 minutes or until tender. Add beans, tomatoes, corn and taco seasoning mix; bring to a boil over high heat. Reduce heat to low; simmer 5 minutes.

**3.** Place two tortillas side by side in prepared baking dish. Top each tortilla with about ½ cup bean mixture; sprinkle with one third of cheese. Repeat layers twice. Pour water around edges of tortillas. Cover with foil.

**4.** Bake 30 to 35 minutes or until heated through. Cut into wedges; serve with sour cream and olives, if desired.                    *Makes 6 servings*

# Caramelized Onion Focaccia

2 tablespoons plus 1 teaspoon olive oil, divided
1 loaf (16 ounces) frozen bread dough, thawed
4 onions, halved and thinly sliced
½ teaspoon salt
2 tablespoons water
1 tablespoon chopped fresh rosemary
¼ teaspoon black pepper
1 cup (4 ounces) shredded fontina cheese
¼ cup grated Parmesan cheese

**1.** Brush 13×9-inch baking pan with 1 teaspoon oil. Roll out dough into 13×9-inch rectangle on lightly floured surface. Place in prepared pan; cover and let rise in warm place 30 minutes.

**2.** Meanwhile, heat remaining 2 tablespoons oil in large skillet over medium-high heat. Add onions and salt; cook 10 minutes or until onions begin to brown, stirring occasionally. Stir in water. Reduce heat to medium; partially cover and cook 20 minutes or until onions are deep golden brown, stirring occasionally. Remove from heat; stir in rosemary and pepper. Set aside.

**3.** Preheat oven to 375°F. Prick dough all over with fork. Sprinkle fontina cheese over dough; top with caramelized onions. Sprinkle with Parmesan cheese.

**4.** Bake 18 to 20 minutes or until golden brown. Remove from pan to wire rack. Cut into pieces; serve warm.                    *Makes 12 servings*

# Greek Spinach and Feta Pie

⅓ cup butter, melted, divided

2 eggs

1 container (15 ounces) ricotta cheese

1 package (10 ounces) frozen chopped spinach, thawed and squeezed dry

1 package (4 ounces) crumbled feta cheese

¾ teaspoon finely grated lemon peel

¼ teaspoon black pepper

⅛ teaspoon ground nutmeg

1 package (16 ounces) frozen phyllo dough, thawed

**1.** Preheat oven to 350°F. Brush 13×9-inch baking dish lightly with some of butter.

**2.** Beat eggs in medium bowl. Stir in ricotta cheese, spinach, feta cheese, lemon peel, pepper and nutmeg.

**3.** Remove eight sheets of phyllo dough from package. (Reserve remaining dough for another use.) Cut in half crosswise to form 16 rectangles. Cover dough with damp cloth or plastic wrap to prevent drying out.

**4.** Place one piece of dough in prepared dish; brush lightly with some of butter. Top with second piece of dough; brush lightly with butter. Continue layering with six pieces of dough, brushing each with butter. Spread spinach mixture evenly over dough.

**5.** Top spinach mixture with one piece of dough; brush lightly with butter. Repeat layering with remaining seven pieces of dough, brushing each with butter.

**6.** Bake 35 to 40 minutes or until golden brown. *Makes 6 servings*

# Polenta Lasagna

4¼ cups water, divided

1½ cups yellow cornmeal

4 teaspoons finely chopped fresh marjoram

2 medium red bell peppers, chopped

1 teaspoon olive oil

1 pound mushrooms, sliced

1 cup chopped leeks

1 clove garlic, minced

½ cup (2 ounces) shredded mozzarella cheese

2 tablespoons chopped fresh basil

1 tablespoon chopped fresh oregano

⅛ teaspoon black pepper

¼ cup freshly grated Parmesan cheese, divided

**1.** Bring 4 cups water to a boil in medium saucepan over high heat. Slowly add cornmeal, stirring constantly. Reduce heat to low; stir in marjoram. Simmer 15 to 20 minutes or until polenta thickens and pulls away from side of pan. Spread in ungreased 13×9-inch baking pan. Cover and refrigerate about 1 hour or until firm.

**2.** Preheat oven to 350°F. Spray 11×7-inch baking dish with nonstick cooking spray. Place bell peppers and remaining ¼ cup water in food processor or blender; process until smooth.

**3.** Heat oil in medium nonstick skillet over medium heat. Add mushrooms, leeks and garlic; cook and stir 5 minutes or until leeks are crisp-tender. Stir in mozzarella cheese, basil, oregano and black pepper.

**4.** Cut cold polenta into 12 (3½-inch) squares; arrange six squares in prepared baking dish. Spread with half of bell pepper mixture, half of vegetable mixture and 2 tablespoons Parmesan cheese. Top with remaining six squares of polenta, remaining bell pepper and vegetable mixtures and Parmesan cheese.

**5.** Bake 20 minutes or until cheese is melted and polenta is golden brown.

*Makes 6 servings*

# No Frying Eggplant Parmesan

  2 cups plain dry bread crumbs
1½ cups grated Parmesan cheese, divided
  ½ teaspoon Italian seasoning
  ¼ teaspoon garlic powder
  2 medium eggplants (about 2 pounds), peeled and cut into ¼-inch slices
  4 eggs, beaten with 3 tablespoons water
  1 jar (1 pound 10 ounces) RAGÚ® ROBUSTO!® Pasta Sauce
1½ cups shredded part-skim mozzarella cheese (about 6 ounces)

**1.** Preheat oven to 350°F. Combine bread crumbs with ½ cup Parmesan cheese, Italian seasoning and garlic powder in medium bowl. Dip eggplant slices in egg mixture, then bread crumb mixture. Arrange eggplant slices in single layer on lightly oiled baking sheets. Bake 25 minutes or until eggplant is golden.

**2.** Evenly spread 1 cup Pasta Sauce in 13×9-inch baking dish. Layer ½ of the baked eggplant slices, then 1 cup Sauce and ½ cup Parmesan cheese; repeat layers. Cover with aluminum foil and bake 45 minutes. Remove foil and sprinkle with mozzarella cheese. Bake uncovered an additional 10 minutes or until cheese is melted.                    *Makes 6 servings*

**Prep Time:** 10 minutes
**Cook Time:** 1 hour 20 minutes

**Tip:** Get your kids to eat more veggies by letting them help. Breading the eggplant slices is a great way to make veggies fun.

# Fruited Corn Pudding

   5  cups thawed frozen corn, divided
   5  eggs
   ½  cup milk
1 ½  cups whipping cream
   ⅓  cup butter, melted
   1  teaspoon vanilla
   ½  teaspoon salt
   ¼  teaspoon ground nutmeg
   3  tablespoons finely chopped dried apricots
   3  tablespoons dried cranberries or raisins
   3  tablespoons finely chopped dates
   2  tablespoons finely chopped dried pears or other dried fruit

**1.** Preheat oven to 350°F. Spray 13×9-inch baking dish with nonstick cooking spray.

**2.** Combine 3½ cups corn, eggs and milk in food processor; process until almost smooth. Pour into large bowl.

**3.** Stir in cream, butter, vanilla, salt and nutmeg until well blended. Add remaining 1½ cups corn, apricots, cranberries, dates and pears; mix well. Pour into prepared baking dish.

**4.** Bake 50 to 60 minutes or until center is set and top begins to brown. Let stand 10 to 15 minutes before serving.          *Makes 8 servings*

# Spinach Stuffed Manicotti

   8  uncooked manicotti pasta shells
½  tablespoon olive oil
   1  teaspoon dried rosemary
   1  teaspoon dried sage
   1  teaspoon dried oregano
   1  teaspoon dried thyme
   1  teaspoon minced garlic
1½  cups chopped fresh tomatoes
   1  package (10 ounces) frozen spinach, thawed and squeezed dry
½  cup ricotta cheese
½  cup fresh whole wheat bread crumbs
   2  egg whites, lightly beaten

**1.** Cook pasta according to package directions. Drain and rinse under cold running water until cool enough to handle.

**2.** Preheat oven to 350°F. Heat oil in medium saucepan over medium heat. Add rosemary, sage, oregano, thyme and garlic; cook and stir 1 minute. Stir in tomatoes; simmer over low heat 10 minutes, stirring occasionally.

**3.** Combine spinach, ricotta cheese and bread crumbs in medium bowl; mix well. Fold in egg whites. Fill pasta shells with spinach mixture.

**4.** Pour one third of tomato mixture into 13×9-inch baking dish. Arrange manicotti in dish; pour remaining tomato mixture over top. Cover with foil.

**5.** Bake 30 minutes or until hot and bubbly.    *Makes 4 servings*

# Root Vegetable Gratin

3 tablespoons unsalted butter, softened

1 small butternut squash (about 1½ pounds), peeled and thinly sliced (about 4 cups)

1 pound red potatoes, peeled and thinly sliced (about 3 cups)

1 bulb celery root (celeriac), about 1 pound, peeled, cut in half and thinly sliced (about 1 cup)

1 bunch leeks, washed well, white part only, thinly sliced (about 1 cup)

1¾ cups SWANSON® Vegetable Broth (Regular **or** Certified Organic)

½ cup heavy cream

1 teaspoon minced fresh thyme leaves

½ teaspoon ground nutmeg

⅓ cup grated Parmesan cheese

**1.** Heat the oven to 400°F. Spread the butter in a 13×9×2-inch baking dish. Add the squash, potatoes, celery root and leeks to the prepared dish.

**2.** Heat the broth, cream, thyme and nutmeg in a 2-quart saucepan over medium heat to a boil. Season to taste.

**3.** Pour the broth mixture over the vegetables and toss to coat.

**4.** Bake for 25 minutes. Reduce the temperature to 350°F. and bake for 40 minutes more or until golden brown and the vegetables are tender. (If the vegetables are browning too fast in the first 25 minutes, cover the dish loosely with foil.)

**5.** Sprinkle with the cheese. Let stand for 10 minutes.        *Makes 6 servings*

**Kitchen Tip:** Use a mandoline to slice the potatoes to a ⅛-inch thickness.

## Apple Cake

2½ cups all-purpose flour
 2 teaspoons ground cinnamon, divided
 1 teaspoon baking powder
 1 teaspoon baking soda
 1 teaspoon salt
 ¼ teaspoon ground nutmeg
1¼ cups granulated sugar, divided
 1 cup (2 sticks) butter, softened
 ¾ cup packed brown sugar
 2 eggs
 1 teaspoon vanilla
 1 cup buttermilk
 3 cups chopped peeled apples
 1 cup chopped nuts

**1.** Preheat oven to 350°F. Spray 13×9-inch baking pan with nonstick cooking spray.

**2.** Combine flour, 1 teaspoon cinnamon, baking powder, baking soda, salt and nutmeg in medium bowl. Beat ¾ cup granulated sugar, butter and brown sugar in large bowl with electric mixer at medium speed 3 minutes or until light and fluffy. Beat in eggs and vanilla. Beat in buttermilk until blended. Add flour mixture; beat until blended. Stir in apples. Pour batter into prepared pan.

**3.** Combine remaining ½ cup granulated sugar, 1 teaspoon cinnamon and nuts in small bowl; sprinkle over batter.

**4.** Bake 35 to 40 minutes or until toothpick inserted in center comes out clean. Cool completely in pan on wire rack.       *Makes 12 to 16 servings*

# Simply Dreamy Cherry Cheesecake

2 cups graham cracker crumbs

½ cup (1 stick) butter, melted

1 package (4-serving size) cheesecake instant pudding and pie filling mix

2 cups milk

4 cups thawed frozen whipped topping, divided

1 can (21 ounces) cherry pie filling

**1.** Combine graham cracker crumbs and butter in medium bowl; mix well. Press into bottom of 13×9-inch baking pan.

**2.** Whisk milk into pudding mix in medium bowl until well blended. Fold in 2 cups whipped topping. Spread over crust.

**3.** Spread pie filling over pudding mixture. Carefully spread remaining 2 cups whipped topping over pie filling. Refrigerate 2 hours or until chilled.

*Makes 12 to 16 servings*

# Frosted Spiced Sweet Potato Cake

1½ cups all-purpose flour

1¼ cups granulated sugar

2 teaspoons baking powder

1 teaspoon ground cinnamon

½ teaspoon baking soda

½ teaspoon salt

¼ teaspoon ground allspice

2 cups mashed cooked sweet potatoes

¾ cup canola oil

2 eggs

½ cup chopped walnuts or pecans, plus additional for garnish

½ cup raisins

Cream Cheese Frosting (recipe follows)

**1.** Preheat oven to 325°F. Spray 13×9-inch baking pan with nonstick cooking spray

**2.** Combine flour, granulated sugar, baking powder, cinnamon, baking soda, salt and allspice in medium bowl. Beat sweet potatoes, oil and eggs in large bowl with electric mixer at low speed until blended. Add flour mixture; beat at medium speed 30 seconds or until well blended. Stir in ½ cup walnuts and raisins. Pour batter into prepared pan.

**3.** Bake 35 minutes or until toothpick inserted into center comes out clean. Cool completely in pan on wire rack.

**4.** Prepare Cream Cheese Frosting. Spread frosting over cake; sprinkle with additional walnuts. *Makes 12 to 16 servings*

**Cream Cheese Frosting:** Beat 1 package (8 ounces) softened cream cheese, ¼ cup (½ stick) softened butter and ¼ teaspoon salt in medium bowl with electric mixer at medium-high speed until light and fluffy. Add 1½ cups sifted powdered sugar, ¼ cup at a time; beat until well blended. Stir in ¼ teaspoon vanilla.

# Classic Chocolate Cake

2 cups all-purpose flour

⅔ cup unsweetened cocoa powder

1¼ teaspoons baking soda

1 teaspoon salt

¼ teaspoon baking powder

1 cup granulated sugar

¾ cup (1½ sticks) butter, softened

⅔ cup packed brown sugar

3 eggs

1 teaspoon vanilla

1⅓ cups water

Prepared chocolate frosting (optional)

**1.** Preheat oven to 350°F. Spray 13×9-inch baking pan with nonstick cooking spray.

**2.** Combine flour, cocoa, baking soda, salt and baking powder in medium bowl. Beat granulated sugar, butter and brown sugar in large bowl with electric mixer at medium-high speed 2 minutes or until light and fluffy. Add eggs and vanilla; beat 2 minutes. Add flour mixture alternately with water; beat just until blended. Pour batter into prepared pan.

**3.** Bake 25 to 35 minutes or until toothpick inserted into center comes out clean. Cool completely in pan on wire rack. Frost cake, if desired.

*Makes about 12 to 16 servings*

# Apple Toffee Crisp

          5  cups peeled and sliced Granny Smith apples (about 5 medium apples)
          5  cups peeled and sliced McIntosh apples (about 5 medium apples)
      1¼  cups sugar, divided
      1¼  cups all-purpose flour, divided
        ¾  cup (1½ sticks) butter or margarine, divided
      1⅓  cups (8-ounce package) HEATH® BITS 'O BRICKLE® Toffee Bits
          1  cup uncooked rolled oats
        ½  teaspoon ground cinnamon
        ¼  teaspoon baking powder
        ¼  teaspoon baking soda
        ¼  teaspoon salt
             Whipped topping or ice cream (optional)

**1.** Heat oven to 375°F. Grease 13×9×2-inch baking pan.

**2.** Toss apple slices, ¾ cup sugar and ¼ cup flour in large bowl, coating apples evenly. Spread in bottom of prepared pan. Dot with ¼ cup (½ stick) butter.

**3.** Stir together toffee bits, oats, remaining ½ cup sugar, remaining 1 cup flour, cinnamon, baking powder, baking soda and salt in medium bowl. Melt remaining ½ cup (1 stick) butter; add to oat mixture, mixing until crumbs are formed. Sprinkle crumb mixture over apples.

**4.** Bake 45 to 50 minutes or until topping is lightly browned and apples are tender. Serve warm with whipped topping or ice cream, if desired. Cover; refrigerate leftovers.                    *Makes 10 to 12 servings*

# Favorite Potluck Carrot Cake

1 package (about 15 ounces) yellow cake mix without pudding in the mix

1 package (4-serving size) vanilla instant pudding and pie filling mix

3 cups grated carrots

1 can (8 ounces) crushed pineapple, undrained

4 eggs

½ cup chopped walnuts

½ cup water

2 teaspoons ground cinnamon

2 packages (8 ounces each) cream cheese, softened

½ cup (1 stick) butter, softened

2 teaspoons vanilla

2 cups powdered sugar, sifted

**1.** Preheat oven to 350°F. Spray 13×9-inch baking pan with nonstick cooking spray.

**2.** Beat cake mix, pudding mix, carrots, pineapple, eggs, walnuts, water and cinnamon in large bowl with electric mixer at low speed 30 seconds. Beat at medium speed 2 minutes. Pour batter into prepared pan.

**3.** Bake 40 to 45 minutes or until toothpick inserted into center comes out clean. Cool completely in pan on wire rack.

**4.** Beat cream cheese, butter and vanilla in medium bowl with electric mixer at medium-high speed 2 minutes or until fluffy. Gradually add powdered sugar, beating until well blended and creamy. Spread over top of cake.

*Makes 12 to 16 servings*

# Double Peanut Butter Snack Cake

Peanut Butter Topping (recipe follows)
1 cup all-purpose flour
1 cup whole wheat flour
1½ teaspoons baking powder
¾ teaspoon baking soda
½ teaspoon salt
¾ cup honey
½ cup (1 stick) butter, softened
¼ cup creamy peanut butter
2 eggs
1½ teaspoons vanilla
¾ cup buttermilk

**1.** Prepare Peanut Butter Topping.

**2.** Preheat oven to 350°F. Spray 13×9-inch baking pan with nonstick cooking spray; dust lightly with flour.

**3.** Combine all-purpose flour, whole wheat flour, baking powder, baking soda and salt in medium bowl. Beat honey, butter and peanut butter in large bowl with electric mixer at medium speed until creamy. Beat in eggs and vanilla until well blended. Add flour mixture alternately with buttermilk, beating until blended after each addition. Pour batter into prepared pan. Crumble topping over batter.

**4.** Bake 25 to 30 minutes or until toothpick inserted into center comes out clean. Serve warm or cool completely.     *Makes 12 to 16 servings*

**Peanut Butter Topping:** Combine ¾ cup granulated sugar, ½ cup creamy peanut butter and 2 tablespoons all-purpose flour in medium bowl; mix well. Stir in 1 cup milk chocolate chips and ½ cup finely chopped pecans until blended.

# Blueberry Cinnamon Dump Cake

2 packages (12 ounces each) frozen blueberries, thawed and drained *or* 4½ cups fresh blueberries

⅓ cup sugar

¾ teaspoon ground cinnamon, divided

1 package (about 15 ounces) yellow cake mix

¾ cup (1½ sticks) butter, cut into thin slices

Ice cream (optional)

**1.** Preheat oven to 350°F. Spray 13×9-inch baking pan with nonstick cooking spray.

**2.** Spread blueberries in prepared pan. Sprinkle with sugar and ½ teaspoon cinnamon; toss to coat. Top with cake mix, spreading evenly. Top with butter in single layer, covering cake mix as much as possible. Sprinkle with remaining ¼ teaspoon cinnamon.

**3.** Bake 50 to 60 minutes or until toothpick inserted into center of cake comes out clean. Cool at least 15 minutes before serving. Serve with ice cream, if desired. *Makes 12 to 16 servings*

# Cranberry Bread Pudding

4 cups milk

2 cups sugar

5 eggs, lightly beaten

1 cup dried cranberries

2 tablespoons vanilla

1 tablespoon baking powder

½ teaspoon ground cinnamon

1 loaf (16 ounces) French bread, cut into cubes

## Brandy Sauce

1½ cups sugar

1 cup (2 sticks) butter

½ cup milk

½ to ¾ cup brandy

**1.** Preheat oven to 350°F. Spray 13×9-inch baking dish with nonstick cooking spray.

**2.** Combine 4 cups milk, 2 cups sugar, eggs, cranberries,, vanilla, baking powder and cinnamon in large bowl; mix well. Add bread; toss to coat. Pour into prepared baking dish.

**3.** Bake 50 to 70 minutes or until golden brown and knife inserted into center comes out clean.

**4.** For sauce, combine 1½ cups sugar, butter and ½ cup milk in medium saucepan; heat over medium-high heat until butter melts and sugar dissolves, stirring frequently. Remove from heat; stir in brandy. Serve with bread pudding.                    *Makes 12 to 16 servings*

# Oat-Apricot Snack Cake

1 container (6 ounces) plain yogurt (not fat free)
¾ cup packed brown sugar
½ cup granulated sugar
⅓ cup vegetable oil
1 egg
¼ cup milk, divided
2 teaspoons vanilla
1 cup all-purpose flour
½ cup whole wheat flour
1 teaspoon baking soda
1 teaspoon ground cinnamon
½ teaspoon salt
2 cups old-fashioned oats
1 cup (about 6 ounces) chopped dried apricots
1 cup powdered sugar

**1.** Preheat oven to 350°F. Spray 13×9-inch baking pan with nonstick cooking spray.

**2.** Combine yogurt, brown sugar, granulated sugar, oil, egg, 2 tablespoons milk and vanilla in large bowl until well blended. Sift all-purpose flour, whole wheat flour, baking soda, cinnamon and salt into medium bowl. Add to yogurt mixture; stir until blended. Stir in oats and apricots until well blended. Spread batter in prepared pan.

**3.** Bake 25 to 30 minutes or until toothpick inserted into center comes out clean. Cool completely in pan on wire rack.

**4.** Whisk powdered sugar and remaining 2 tablespoons milk in small bowl until smooth. Spoon glaze into small resealable food storage bag; seal bag. Cut ¼ inch from one corner; drizzle glaze over cake.    *Makes 24 servings*

# Nancy's Tiramisù

6 egg yolks
1¼ cups sugar
1½ cups mascarpone cheese
1¾ cups whipping cream, beaten to soft peaks
1¾ cups cold espresso or strong brewed coffee
3 tablespoons brandy
3 tablespoons grappa (optional)
4 packages (3 ounces each) ladyfingers
2 tablespoons unsweetened cocoa powder

**1.** Beat egg yolks and sugar in small bowl with electric mixer at medium-high speed until pale yellow. Place in top of double boiler over simmering water. Cook 10 minutes, stirring constantly. Combine egg yolk mixture and mascarpone cheese in large bowl; beat with electric mixer at low speed until well blended and fluffy. Fold in whipped cream. Set aside.

**2.** Combine espresso, brandy and grappa, if desired, in medium bowl. Dip 24 ladyfingers, one at a time, into espresso mixture and arrange side by side in single layer in 13×9-inch baking dish. (Dip ladyfingers into mixture quickly or they will absorb too much liquid and fall apart.)

**3.** Spread half of mascarpone mixture evenly over ladyfinger layer. Sift 1 tablespoon cocoa over mascarpone layer. Repeat with another layer of 24 ladyfingers dipped in espresso mixture. Cover with remaining mascarpone mixture. Sift remaining 1 tablespoon cocoa over top.

**4.** Refrigerate at least 4 hours or overnight before serving.

*Makes 12 servings*

**Substitution:** If mascarpone cheese is unavailable, combine 1 package (8 ounces) softened cream cheese, ¼ cup sour cream and 2 tablespoons whipping cream in medium bowl. Beat with electric mixer at medium speed 2 minutes or until light and fluffy.

# St. Louis Gooey Butter Cake

1 package (about 15 ounces) yellow cake mix
½ cup (1 stick) butter, melted
4 eggs, divided
1 package (8 ounces) cream cheese, softened
1 teaspoon vanilla
3 cups powdered sugar, plus additional for serving

**1.** Preheat oven to 350°F. Spray 13×9-inch baking pan with nonstick cooking spray.

**2.** Beat cake mix, butter and 2 eggs in large bowl with electric mixer at low speed 1 minute or just until blended. Press evenly onto bottom of prepared pan.

**3.** Beat cream cheese, remaining 2 eggs and vanilla in medium bowl with electric mixer at medium-high speed 2 minutes or until well blended. Gradually add 3 cups powdered sugar; beat until smooth. Spread evenly over cake mix layer in pan.

**4.** Bake 35 to 40 minutes or until top is lightly browned. (Cake will puff up then collapse during baking.) Cool completely in pan on wire rack. Sprinkle with additional powdered sugar, if desired.          *Makes 12 to 16 servings*

# Gingerbread Cheesecake Bars

> 2 cups all-purpose flour
> 1½ teaspoons ground ginger, divided
> 1 teaspoon baking soda
> ¾ teaspoon ground cinnamon
> ¼ teaspoon salt
> ¼ teaspoon ground allspice
> 1 package (8 ounces) cream cheese, softened
> ⅔ cup sugar, divided
> 3 eggs, divided
> ½ teaspoon vanilla
> ½ cup (1 stick) butter, softened
> ¾ cup molasses

**1.** Preheat oven to 350°F. Spray 13×9-inch baking pan with nonstick cooking spray. Combine flour, 1 teaspoon ginger, baking soda, cinnamon, salt and allspice in small bowl.

**2.** Beat cream cheese and ⅓ cup sugar in medium bowl with electric mixer at medium speed until light and fluffy. Add 1 egg, remaining ½ teaspoon ginger and vanilla; beat until well blended and smooth. Refrigerate until ready to use.

**3.** Beat butter and remaining ⅓ cup sugar in large bowl with electric mixer at medium speed until light and fluffy. Add molasses and remaining 2 eggs; beat until well blended. Add flour mixture; beat just until blended. Spread batter in prepared pan. Drop cream cheese mixture by spoonfuls onto batter; gently swirl into batter with knife.

**4.** Bake 25 to 30 minutes or until toothpick inserted into center comes out clean. Cool completely in pan on wire rack. *Makes 24 bars*

# Chocolate Pecan Bars

## Crust

- 1⅓ cups all-purpose flour
- ½ cup (1 stick) butter, softened
- ¼ cup packed brown sugar
- ½ teaspoon salt

## Topping

- ¾ cup light corn syrup
- 3 eggs, lightly beaten
- 2 tablespoons butter, melted
- ½ teaspoon vanilla
- ½ teaspoon almond extract
- ¾ cup milk chocolate chips
- ¾ cup semisweet chocolate chips
- ¾ cup chopped pecans, toasted*
- ¾ cup granulated sugar

*To toast pecans, spread in single layer on baking sheet. Bake in preheated 350°F oven 8 to 10 minutes or until lightly browned, stirring occasionally.*

**1.** Preheat oven to 350°F. Spray 13×9-inch baking pan with nonstick cooking spray.

**2.** For crust, combine flour, softened butter, brown sugar and salt in medium bowl; mix with fork until crumbly. Press onto bottom of prepared pan. Bake 12 to 15 minutes or until lightly browned. Let stand 10 minutes.

**3.** Meanwhile, for topping, combine corn syrup, eggs, melted butter, vanilla and almond extract in large bowl; stir with fork until combined (do not beat). Stir in chocolate chips, pecans and granulated sugar until blended. Pour over baked crust.

**4.** Bake 25 to 30 minutes or until toothpick inserted into center comes out clean. Cool completely in pan on wire rack. *Makes 24 bars*

# White Chip Lemon Streusel Bars

- 1 can (14 ounces) sweetened condensed milk (not evaporated milk)
- ½ cup lemon juice
- 1 teaspoon freshly grated lemon peel
- 2 cups (12-ounce package) HERSHEY®S Premier White Chips, divided
- 1 cup packed light brown sugar
- ⅔ cup butter or margarine, softened
- 1½ cups all-purpose flour
- 1½ cups regular rolled or quick-cooking oats
- ¾ cup toasted pecan pieces*
- 1 teaspoon baking powder
- ½ teaspoon salt
- 1 egg
- ½ teaspoon shortening

*To toast pecans: Heat oven to 350°F. Spread pecans in single layer in shallow baking pan. Bake, stirring occasionally, 7 to 8 minutes or until golden brown; cool.

**1.** Heat oven to 350°F. Lightly grease 13×9×2-inch baking pan. Combine sweetened condensed milk, lemon juice and lemon peel in medium bowl; set aside. Measure out ¼ cup and ⅓ cup white chips; set aside. Add remaining white chips to lemon mixture.

**2.** Beat brown sugar and butter in large bowl with electric mixer on medium speed until well blended. Stir together flour, oats, pecans, baking powder and salt; add to butter mixture, blending well. Set aside 1⅔ cups oats mixture. Add egg to remaining oats mixture, blending until crumbly; press onto bottom of prepared pan. Gently spoon lemon mixture on top, spreading evenly. Add reserved ⅓ cup white chips to reserved oats mixture. Sprinkle over lemon layer, pressing down lightly.

**3.** Bake 20 to 25 minutes or until lightly browned. Cool in pan on wire rack. Place remaining ¼ cup white chips and shortening in small microwave-safe bowl. Microwave at MEDIUM (50%) 30 seconds or until chips are melted and mixture is smooth when stirred. Drizzle over baked bars. Allow drizzle to set; cut into bars. *Makes 24 to 36 bars*

# Chocolate Caramel Brownies

 1  package (18.25 ounces) chocolate cake mix
 1  cup chopped nuts
 ½  cup (1 stick) butter or margarine, melted
 1  cup NESTLÉ® CARNATION® Evaporated Milk, *divided*
 35  caramels, unwrapped (10-ounce package)
 2  cups (12-ounce package) NESTLÉ® TOLL HOUSE®
      Semi-Sweet Chocolate Morsels

**PREHEAT** oven to 350°F.

**COMBINE** cake mix and nuts in large bowl. Stir in butter and ⅔ *cup* evaporated milk (batter will be thick). Spread *half* of batter into greased 13×9-inch baking pan.

**BAKE** for 15 minutes.

**HEAT** caramels and *remaining* evaporated milk in small saucepan over low heat, stirring constantly, until caramels are melted. Sprinkle morsels over brownie; drizzle with caramel mixture.

**DROP** *remaining* batter by heaping teaspoonfuls over caramel mixture.

**BAKE** for 25 to 30 minutes or until center is set. Cool in pan on wire rack.

*Makes 2 dozen brownies*

**Prep Time:** 15 minutes
**Cook Time:** 45 minutes
**Cool Time:** 20 minutes

# Whole Wheat Date Bars

4½ cups chopped dates

2½ cups water

2¾ cups whole wheat flour

2 cups old-fashioned oats

¼ cup all-purpose flour

¼ cup packed brown sugar

1½ teaspoons salt

½ teaspoon ground cinnamon

½ cup maple syrup

½ cup (1 stick) cold butter, cut into small pieces

1 cup vegetable shortening, at room temperature

**1.** Preheat oven to 400°F. Spray 13×9-inch baking dish with nonstick cooking spray.

**2.** Combine dates and water in large saucepan; cook over medium heat 10 minutes or until thickened to jamlike consistency, stirring frequently. Remove from heat.

**3.** Combine whole wheat flour, oats, all-purpose flour, brown sugar, salt and cinnamon in large bowl; mix well. Stir in maple syrup. Cut in butter with pastry blender or two knives until mixture resembles coarse crumbs. Stir in shortening until dough holds together.

**4.** Place 5 cups dough in prepared baking dish; press firmly onto bottom and partially up sides of dish to form crust. Pour date mixture evenly into crust; top with remaining dough.

**5.** Bake 25 minutes or until golden brown. Cool completely in pan on wire rack.

*Makes 2 dozen bars*

# Southern Caramel Apple Bars

2 cups all-purpose flour

1 teaspoon salt

½ teaspoon baking powder

½ teaspoon baking soda

⅔ cup butter

¾ cup packed brown sugar

½ cup granulated sugar

1 egg

1 teaspoon vanilla

4 Granny Smith apples, peeled and coarsely chopped

½ cup pecans, chopped

24 caramel candies, unwrapped

2 tablespoons milk

**1.** Preheat oven to 350°F. Spray 13×9-inch baking dish with nonstick cooking spray.

**2.** Combine flour, salt, baking powder and baking soda in medium bowl. Melt butter in medium saucepan over medium heat. Remove from heat; stir in brown sugar and granulated sugar. Add egg and vanilla; stir until well blended. Add flour mixture; mix well. Press onto bottom of prepared baking dish; top with apples.

**3.** Bake 40 to 45 minutes or until edges are browned and pulling away from sides of pan. Cool completely in pan on wire rack.

**4.** Toast pecans in medium nonstick skillet over medium-high heat 2 minutes or until fragrant, stirring constantly. Remove to small bowl. Wipe out skillet with paper towel. Heat caramels and milk in same skillet over medium-low heat until melted and smooth, stirring constantly.

**5.** Drizzle caramel sauce over cooled apple bars; sprinkle with pecans. Let stand 30 minutes. *Makes about 24 bars*

# Not-So-Sinful Brownies

¼ cup vegetable oil
3 squares (1 ounce each) unsweetened chocolate
1 ¼ cups granulated sugar
½ cup applesauce
4 egg whites or 2 eggs, lightly beaten
1 teaspoon vanilla
1 cup QUAKER® Oats (quick or old fashioned, uncooked)
1 cup all-purpose flour
1 teaspoon baking powder
¼ teaspoon salt (optional)
1 tablespoon powdered sugar

**1.** Heat oven to 350°F. Lightly spray bottom of 13×9-inch baking pan with nonstick cooking spray.

**2.** Heat oil and chocolate in large saucepan over low heat until chocolate is melted, stirring frequently. Remove from heat. Stir in granulated sugar and applesauce until sugar is dissolved. Stir in egg whites and vanilla until completely blended. Add combined oats, flour, baking powder and salt, if desired; mix well. Spread evenly into pan.

**3.** Bake 22 to 25 minutes or until edges begin to pull away from sides of pan. Cool completely in pan on wire rack. Cut into bars. Store tightly covered. Sprinkle with powdered sugar just before serving.          *Makes 24 brownies*

# Raspberry Almond Squares

1 package (about 15 ounces) yellow cake mix
½ cup sliced almonds, coarsely chopped
½ cup (1 stick) butter, melted
1 jar (12 ounces) seedless raspberry jam
1 package (8 ounces) cream cheese, softened
1 egg
2 tablespoons all-purpose flour

**1.** Preheat oven to 350°F. Line 13×9-inch baking pan with foil, allowing 2-inch overhang around all sides.

**2.** Beat cake mix, almonds and butter in large bowl with electric mixer at medium speed until crumbly. Reserve 1 cup mixture; press remaining mixture into bottom of prepared pan. Bake 10 to 12 minutes or until light golden brown. Cool in pan on wire rack.

**3.** Spread jam evenly over crust. Beat cream cheese, egg and flour in medium bowl with electric mixer at medium speed until blended. Spread over jam; top with reserved crumb mixture.

**4.** Bake 18 to 20 minutes or until golden brown. Cool completely in pan on wire rack.                                                    *Makes 24 bars*

# Peanut Butter Fudge Brownie Bars

1½ cups sugar

1 cup (2 sticks) butter or margarine, melted

2 eggs

1 teaspoon vanilla extract

1¼ cups all-purpose flour

⅔ cup HERSHEY'S Cocoa

¼ cup milk

1¼ cups chopped pecans or walnuts, divided

½ cup (1 stick) butter or margarine

1⅔ cups (10-ounce package) REESE'S® Peanut Butter Chips

1 can (14 ounces) sweetened condensed milk (not evaporated milk)

¼ cup HERSHEY'S SPECIAL DARK® Chocolate Chips or HERSHEY'S Semi-Sweet Chocolate Chips

**1.** Heat oven to 350°F. Grease 13×9×2-inch baking pan.

**2.** Beat sugar, melted butter, eggs and vanilla in large bowl with electric mixer on medium speed until well blended. Add flour, cocoa and milk; beat until blended. Stir in 1 cup nuts. Spread in prepared pan.

**3.** Bake 25 to 30 minutes or just until edges begin to pull away from sides of pan. Cool completely in pan on wire rack.

**4.** Melt ½ cup butter and peanut butter chips in medium saucepan over low heat, stirring constantly. Add sweetened condensed milk, stirring until smooth; pour over baked layer.

**5.** Place chocolate chips in small microwave-safe bowl. Microwave at MEDIUM (50%) 45 seconds or just until chips are melted when stirred. Drizzle bars with melted chocolate; sprinkle with remaining ¼ cup nuts. Refrigerate 1 hour or until firm. Cut into bars. Cover; refrigerate leftover bars. *Makes 24 to 36 bars*

# Mocha Cinnamon Blondies

1 cup all-purpose flour

2 teaspoons instant coffee granules

1 teaspoon ground cinnamon

¼ teaspoon salt

1 cup (2 sticks) butter, melted

1¾ cups sugar

4 eggs

1 cup chopped pecans

¾ cup semisweet chocolate chips

**1.** Preheat oven to 350°F. Spray 13×9-inch baking pan with nonstick cooking spray.

**2.** Combine flour, coffee granules, cinnamon and salt in medium bowl. Beat butter, sugar and eggs in large bowl with electric mixer at medium speed until light and fluffy. Add flour mixture; beat at low speed until blended. Stir in pecans and chocolate chips. Spread batter in prepared pan.

**3.** Bake 30 minutes or until edges begin to pull away from sides of pan. Cool completely in pan on wire rack.                    *Makes 24 blondies*

# Nutty S'Mores Bars

2¼ cups graham cracker crumbs (14 whole graham crackers, crushed)

1 cup (2 sticks) butter, melted, divided

3 tablespoons sugar

1 package (about 15 ounces) milk chocolate cake mix

2 eggs

⅓ cup water

1½ cups mini semisweet chocolate chips, divided

4 whole graham crackers, chopped into ½-inch pieces

1 cup mini marshmallows

1 cup roasted salted peanuts

**1.** Preheat oven to 350°F. Line 13×9-inch baking pan with foil; spray with nonstick cooking spray.

**2.** Combine graham cracker crumbs, ½ cup butter and sugar in medium bowl; mix well. Press onto bottom of prepared pan. Bake 10 minutes; cool in pan on wire rack.

**3.** Beat cake mix, remaining ½ cup butter, eggs and water in large bowl with electric mixer at low speed until well blended. Stir in ½ cup chocolate chips. (Batter will be stiff.) Spread evenly over crust. Bake 25 minutes or until toothpick inserted into center comes out clean.

**4.** *Turn oven to broil.* Sprinkle chopped graham crackers, marshmallows, peanuts and remaining 1 cup chocolate chips over bars. Broil 3 minutes or until marshmallows are puffed and lightly browned. Cool completely in pan on wire rack.                                    *Makes 24 bars*

# Chocolate Seven Layer Bars

- 1½ cups finely crushed thin pretzels or pretzel sticks
- ¾ cup (1½ sticks) butter or margarine, melted
- 1 can (14 ounces) sweetened condensed milk (not evaporated milk)
- 1 package (4 ounces) HERSHEY₍S Unsweetened Chocolate Baking Bar, broken into pieces
- 2 cups miniature marshmallows
- 1 cup MOUNDS® Sweetened Coconut Flakes
- 1 cup coarsely chopped pecans
- 1 package (4 ounces) HERSHEY₍S Semi-Sweet Chocolate Baking Bar, broken into pieces
- 1 tablespoon shortening (do not use butter, margarine, spread or oil)

**1.** Heat oven to 350°F. Combine pretzels and melted butter in small bowl; press evenly onto bottom of ungreased 13×9×2-inch baking pan.

**2.** Place sweetened condensed milk and unsweetened chocolate in small microwave-safe bowl. Microwave at MEDIUM (50%) 1 minute; stir. If necessary, microwave at MEDIUM an additional 15 seconds at a time, stirring after each heating, until mixture is melted and smooth when stirred. Carefully pour over pretzel layer in pan. Top with marshmallows, coconut and pecans; press firmly down onto chocolate layer.

**3.** Bake 25 to 30 minutes or until lightly browned. Cool completely in pan on wire rack.

**4.** Place semi-sweet chocolate and shortening in small microwave-safe bowl. Microwave at MEDIUM (50%) 1 minute or until chocolate is melted when stirred. Drizzle over entire top. Cut into bars. Refrigerate 15 minutes or until glaze is set.

*Makes 36 bars*

# INDEX

# ACKNOWLEDGMENTS

The publisher would like to thank the companies and organizations listed below for the use of their recipes and photographs in this publication.

Campbell Soup Company

Cream of Wheat® Cereal, A Division of B&G Foods North America, Inc.

The Hershey Company

Nestlé USA

Ortega®, A Division of B&G Foods North America, Inc.

The Quaker® Oatmeal Kitchens

Unilever

# METRIC CONVERSION CHART

## VOLUME MEASUREMENTS (dry)

$1/8$ teaspoon = 0.5 mL
$1/4$ teaspoon = 1 mL
$1/2$ teaspoon = 2 mL
$3/4$ teaspoon = 4 mL
1 teaspoon = 5 mL
1 tablespoon = 15 mL
2 tablespoons = 30 mL
$1/4$ cup = 60 mL
$1/3$ cup = 75 mL
$1/2$ cup = 125 mL
$2/3$ cup = 150 mL
$3/4$ cup = 175 mL
1 cup = 250 mL
2 cups = 1 pint = 500 mL
3 cups = 750 mL
4 cups = 1 quart = 1 L

## VOLUME MEASUREMENTS (fluid)

1 fluid ounce (2 tablespoons) = 30 mL
4 fluid ounces ($1/2$ cup) = 125 mL
8 fluid ounces (1 cup) = 250 mL
12 fluid ounces ($1 1/2$ cups) = 375 mL
16 fluid ounces (2 cups) = 500 mL

## WEIGHTS (mass)

$1/2$ ounce = 15 g
1 ounce = 30 g
3 ounces = 90 g
4 ounces = 120 g
8 ounces = 225 g
10 ounces = 285 g
12 ounces = 360 g
16 ounces = 1 pound = 450 g

## DIMENSIONS

$1/16$ inch = 2 mm
$1/8$ inch = 3 mm
$1/4$ inch = 6 mm
$1/2$ inch = 1.5 cm
$3/4$ inch = 2 cm
1 inch = 2.5 cm

## OVEN TEMPERATURES

250°F = 120°C
275°F = 140°C
300°F = 150°C
325°F = 160°C
350°F = 180°C
375°F = 190°C
400°F = 200°C
425°F = 220°C
450°F = 230°C

## BAKING PAN AND DISH EQUIVALENTS

| Utensil | Size in Inches | Size in Centimeters | Volume | Metric Volume |
|---|---|---|---|---|
| Baking or Cake Pan (square or rectangular) | 8×8×2 | 20×20×5 | 8 cups | 2 L |
| | 9×9×2 | 23×23×5 | 10 cups | 2.5 L |
| | 13×9×2 | 33×23×5 | 12 cups | 3 L |
| Loaf Pan | 8½×4½×2½ | 21×11×6 | 6 cups | 1.5 L |
| | 9×9×3 | 23×13×7 | 8 cups | 2 L |
| Round Layer Cake Pan | 8×1½ | 20×4 | 4 cups | 1 L |
| | 9×1½ | 23×4 | 5 cups | 1.25 L |
| Pie Plate | 8×1½ | 20×4 | 4 cups | 1 L |
| | 9×1½ | 23×4 | 5 cups | 1.25 L |
| Baking Dish or Casserole | | | 1 quart/4 cups | 1 L |
| | | | 1½ quart/6 cups | 1.5 L |
| | | | 2 quart/8 cups | 2 L |
| | | | 3 quart/12 cups | 3 L |